MICROMATIC

BUSINESS MANAGEMENT

SIMULATION

GETTING STARTED USER GUIDE

Timothy W. Scott
Minnesota State University, Mankato, Minnesota

John A. Kaliski
Minnesota State University, Mankato, Minnesota

Philip H. Anderson
University of St. Thomas

A.J. Strickland
University of Alabama

Vice President and Publisher: George T. Hoffman
Senior Sponsoring Editor: Lisé Johnson
Senior Content Manager: Damaris R. Curran
Senior Marketing Manager: Steven W. Mikels

Printed in the U.S.A.

ISBN: 0-618-64178-5

Introduction

In this guide, we specify the computer requirements for using *Micromatic*. We also tell you how to login and register so that you can use the *Micromatic* software.

Equipment Needed

In order to use the *Micromatic* web programs, you will need a computer with Internet Explorer version 6.0 (with Service Pack 1) or higher that is connected to the internet. If you experience difficulty opening the program, you may have to turn off any "pop-up" blockers and configure your browser to accept cookies. Finally, although optional, we advise that you use a printer so that you can generate printouts of your quarterly results.

Preparing To Register

You need *two* items before you can register to use the *Micromatic* programs.

1. **A validation code provided by your instructor.** The company code will assign you to the proper industry for the Team version of *Micromatic*. Even if you will not be using the Team version, you need a validation code to create your data file on the server's *Micromatic* database.

2. **Proof of purchase.** You can pay to access *Micromatic* in one of two ways.

    a. Use a credit card to pay online as part of the registration process.

    b. Purchase this Getting Started User's Guide, including a valid Passkey, through a bookstore. You will need to do this *prior* to beginning the registration process. *Please note that if the activation number you use has been used previously, it is invalid. You will NOT be able to use it to register for using the programs!*

6. To register for the correct game, first select either the letter of the alphabet for your institution (e.g., "W" for University of Wisconsin") or enter your instructor's surname (See Exhibit 3). If your instructor has more than one simulation game operating, make sure you select the correct one.

Exhibit 3

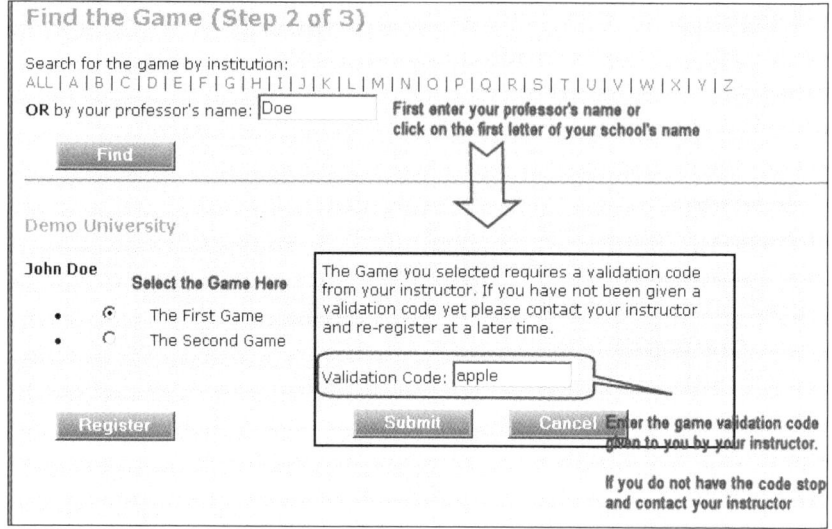

7. Now click on the "Register" button. A pop-up box will appear asking you to enter a validation code. Enter the validation code your instructor gave you and click on "Submit". As noted in Exhibit 4, if you do not have the validation code, you need to contact your instructor before you can proceed any further.

Exhibit 4

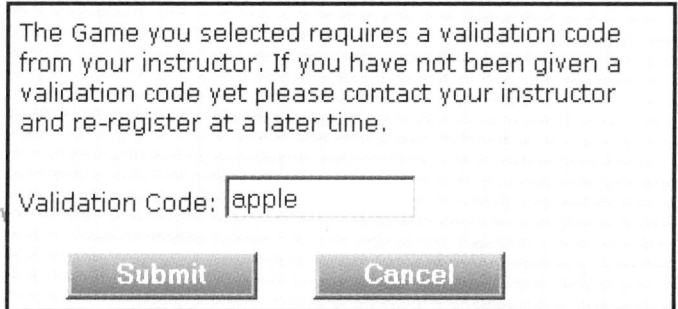

The Game you selected requires a validation code from your instructor. If you have not been given a validation code yet please contact your instructor and re-register at a later time.

Validation Code: apple

Submit   Cancel

8. After you click on the Register button, a screen like that shown in Exhibit 5 will appear on your monitor. To complete your registration for *Micromatic*, you need to pay for your *Micromatic* account by either (a) entering a Passkey to provide proof of payment that you purchased *Micromatic* bundled with a textbook or (b) doing a direct purchase using PayPal.

    a. If you purchased *Micromatic* with a textbook, enter the validation code (located on the back page of this guidebook) and select Enter (See left arrow in Exhibit 5). Go to Step 11, next.

    b. To purchase *Micromatic* using PayPal, click on the PayPal icon (See right arrow in Exhibit 5).

Exhibit 5

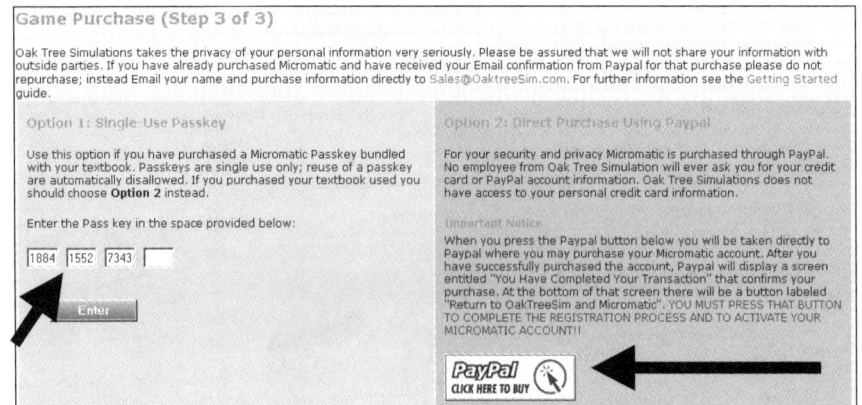

9. If you already have a PayPal account, enter your email address and password, as shown in Exhibit 6. If you do not have a PayPal account, you can open one by clicking on the "Continue Checkout" button shown in Exhibit 6.

Exhibit 6

10. After you enter the information required by PayPal, you will see a screen like that shown in Exhibit 7. Next, click on the button in the lower right-hand corner of the screen to return to the *Micromatic* web site.

Exhibit 7

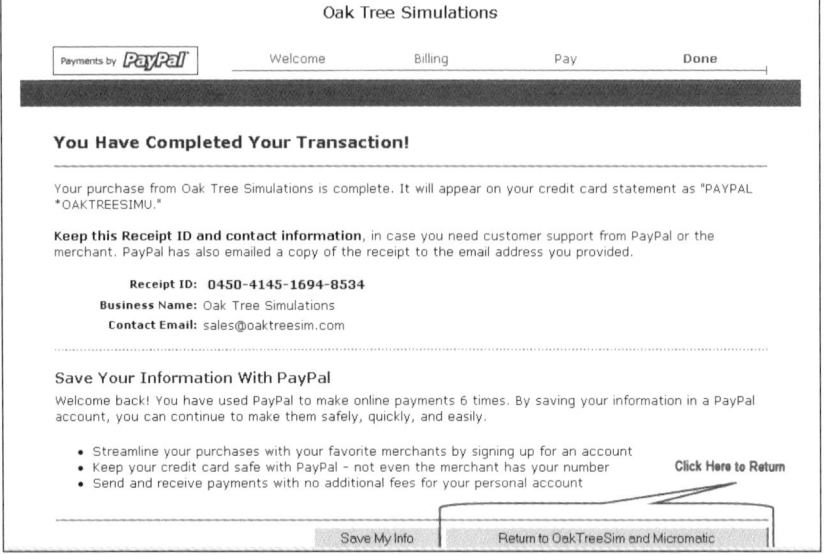

11. A screen similar to that shown in Exhibit 8 will appear on your monitor. Select the correct team to join by using the dialog box at the bottom of the screen (See left arrow in Exhibit 8). Your name will be entered with the proper team.

Exhibit 8

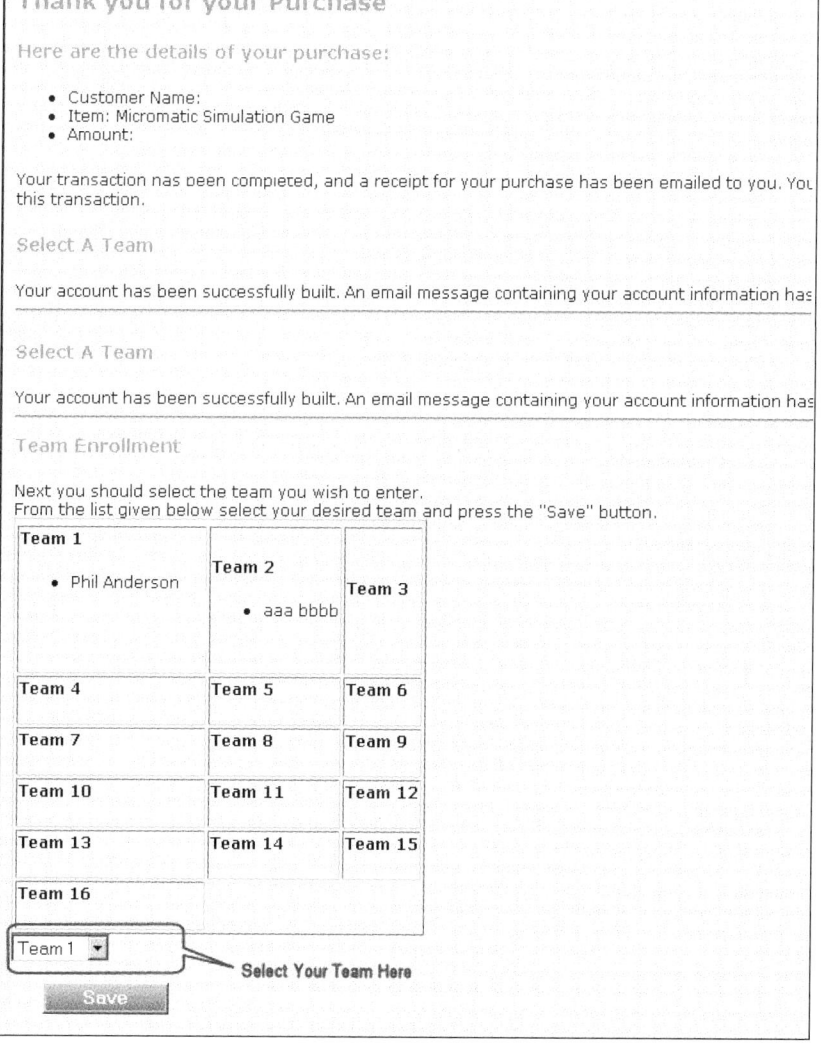

12. You can now begin working with your *Micromatic* program by clicking on the icon for the game you wish to play, *Micromatic* Team or Solo (see Exhibit 9).

Exhibit 9

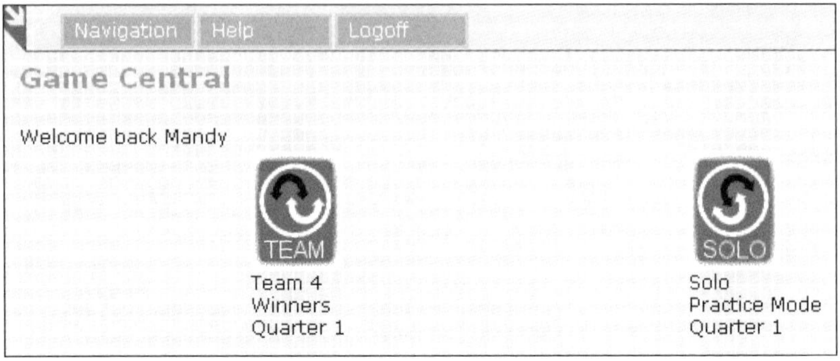

Use the Game Central screen to switch between using the Team game and the Solo game.

Account Maintenance

You will use this screen to make changes to your *Micromatic* account data. Do this by clicking on the Navigation menu option. Then select the Account Maintenance option. A screen like that shown in Exhibit 10 will appear on your monitor.

Exhibit 10

Account Maintenance

Update the account settings below:

First name   Josh
Middle name
Last name   Jones
Email   jjones@nowher
Desired Language English
Password
Confirm Password
*Leave password and confirm password blank if no change is desired.

Save   Cancel

Change Email Address

This option allows you to change the email address from the one you initially entered when registering to use *Micromatic* to a new one. To do this, type in your new email address and select "Save".

Change Email Address

This option allows you to change the email address from the one you initially entered when registering to use *Micromatic* to a new one. To do this, type in your new email address and select "Save".

Change Password

You may decide, for security reasons, to change your company's password. This option allows you to make that change. You can change your password as often as you wish, but be careful. It is usually advisable not to select as a password the name of a family member or a nickname that others are likely to guess. Also, frequent changes can lead to confusion. If you forget your password you will not be able to access your files to make decisions for the upcoming quarter of operation. If this happens, see your instructor for help.

13